ALIEN ABDUCTIONS

BY RAY McCLELLAN

EPIC

BELLWETHER MEDIA · MINNEAPOLIS, MN

EPIC BOOKS are no ordinary books. They burst with intense action, high-speed heroics, and shadows of the unknown. Are you ready for an Epic adventure?

This edition first published in 2014 by Bellwether Media, Inc.

Library of Congress Cataloging-in-Publication Data

McClellan, Ray.
  Alien Abductions / by Ray McClellan.
    pages cm – (Epic. Unexplained Mysteries)
  Summary: "Engaging images accompany information about alien abductions. The combination of high-interest subject matter and light text is intended for students in grades 2 through 7"– Provided by publisher.
  Audience: Ages 7-12.
  Includes bibliographical references and index.
  ISBN 978-1-62617-100-8 (hardcover : alk. paper)
  1. Alien abduction–Juvenile literature. I. Title.
  BF2050.M378 2014
  001.942–dc23
                        2013035915

Designed by Jon Eppard.

Printed in the United States of America, North Mankato, MN.

TABLE OF CONTENTS

TAKEN?

A farmer wakes up in the middle of the night. A bright light shines through his bedroom window. He goes outside to **investigate**. But the strange glow disappears suddenly.

4

In the morning, the farmer finds a man in his field. The man tells stories about flying with **aliens**. Is the man a crazy **drifter**? Or is he really the **victim** of an alien **abduction**?

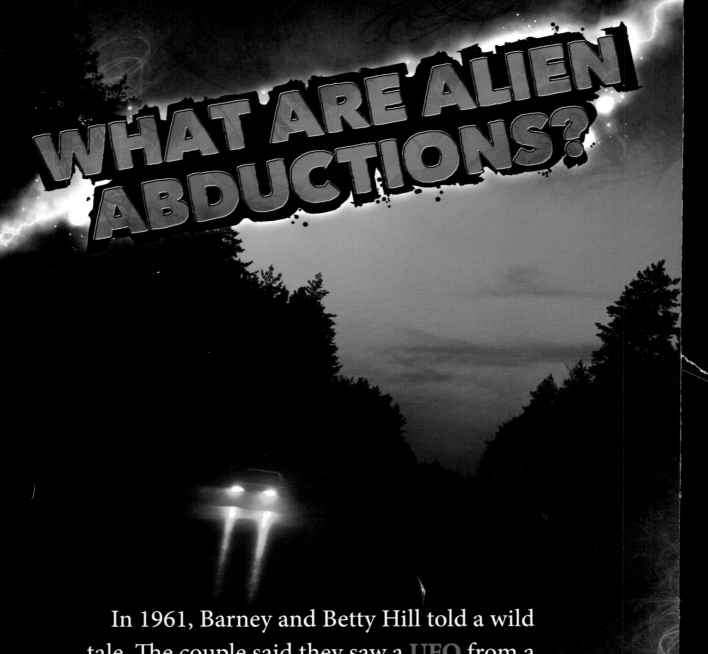

WHAT ARE ALIEN ABDUCTIONS?

In 1961, Barney and Betty Hill told a wild tale. The couple said they saw a **UFO** from a New Hampshire road. They claimed aliens took them aboard a spaceship.

THE FIRST OF MANY

The Hills' story was the first popular claim of an alien abduction.

Since then, people around the world have reported similar stories. Many see lights in the sky. Some say they were part of medical experiments. Others report **missing time**.

The aliens in most of the stories are called the Grays. They are short and skinny with large heads and gray skin.

COMMON CHARACTERISTICS OF THE GRAYS

- dark gray skin
- large head
- large black eyes
- small mouth
- no ears
- skinny body
- long arms
- short legs

THE REAL STORY?

ANCIENT BELIEFS

Many alien researchers believe ancient humans were in contact with aliens. They think people worshipped them as gods.

Some believers think the Grays take people for medical experiments. Others think aliens come to Earth to warn us of danger.

Most skeptics think the stories are hoaxes. They believe the victims are trying to trick them.

Others think that alien abductions are **hallucinations** or dreams. They believe victims imagine things that are not real.

There is a lot left to explore in space. No one knows for sure if humans are alone. Do aliens really visit Earth? Or do our minds invent these stories?

GLOSSARY

abduction—an event in which someone is captured against his or her will

aliens—beings from another planet

drifter—a person who travels from place to place with no plan

hallucinations—experiences of seeing or hearing things that are not really there

hoaxes—attempts to trick people into believing something

investigate—to search for clues to find out the facts about something

missing time—time that a person cannot remember

skeptics—people who doubt the truth of something

UFO—a mysterious object moving in the sky; UFO stands for "unidentified flying object."

victim—a person who has been the target of a harmful act

TO LEARN MORE

At the Library

Erickson, Justin. *Alien Abductions*. Minneapolis, Minn.: Bellwether Media, 2011.

Higgins, Nadia. *UFOs*. Minneapolis, Minn.: Bellwether Media, 2014.

Martin, Michael. *The Unsolved Mystery of Alien Abductions*. North Mankato, Minn.: Capstone Press, 2014.

On the Web

Learning more about alien abductions is as easy as 1, 2, 3.

1. Go to www.factsurfer.com.

2. Enter "alien abductions" into the search box.

3. Click the "Surf" button and you will see a list of related Web sites.

With factsurfer.com, finding more information is just a click away.

INDEX

The images in this book are reproduced through the courtesy of: Fer Gregory, front cover, p. 7 (top); David Trood/ Getty Images, pp. 4-5; Andrew Lever, p. 6; shiva3d, p. 7; axyse, p. 8; Chromatika Multimedia, p. 9 (top); Bettmann/ Corbis/ AP Images, p. 9 (bottom); Kiketxo, p. 10 (composite); Zeppelie, pp. 12-13; ArchieMkDesign, pp. 14, 19, 21; David Levenson/ Alamy, p. 15; Photobank Gallery, p. 16; asiseeit, p. 17; wavebreakmedia, p. 18; infografick peresanz, p. 20 (composite).